Bus Girl

For AmAnda,
Love,
Eva Eason

Summer
2000

" Tears streamed from my eyes as I read the poems in Gretchen's book. To be blessed with a Down's child as I have been, and to realize the accomplishment of achieving a book filled with abstraction and conceptualization just stunned me. God bless Gretchen for her efforts and for helping people grasp the fact that people with Down syndrome can contribute to society in an artistic capacity as well as in the labor force, and that Down's people are just that ... people."

—JOE DIFFIE

Country singer, Epic Records
(Gretchen's favorite singer)

Bus Girl

Poems by
Gretchen Josephson

Edited by Lula O. Lubchenco
with Allen C. Crocker

BROOKLINE BOOKS

ISBN 1-57129-041-9

Library of Congress Catalog Card Number: 97-74012

Cover design by Roger Gordy.
Book design and typography by Erica L. Schultz.

Printed in Canada by Best Book Manufacturers, Louiseville, Quebec.

5 4 3 2 1

Published by
BROOKLINE BOOKS
P.O. Box 1047
Cambridge, Massachusetts 02238
(617) 868-0360
Order toll-free: 1-800-666-BOOK

Contents

III. VACATIONS & TRAVEL

IV. FAMILY

V. DEATH & GRIEF

VI. FAITH

VII. OTHER POEMS

Acknowledgments

The interest in Gretchen's poems expressed by many friends and professional colleagues has been the force that drove us to make her writings available to a larger audience.

We express our sincere thanks to our extended family for their continuous support and encouragement: first, to Gretchen to continue writing, and then to me, to preserve these poems. Recognizing her talent, Gretchen's sisters, Patty, Johanna, and Karen, put the first ones together as a Christmas gift to the family. The McClain cousins have read and loved them, and encouraged her to continue.

Linda Barth of the Mile High Down Syndrome Association printed some of the poems in their monthly news bulletin, and also spread the word to Margaret Lewis who had some of them printed in *Down Syndrome News*.

Our friends in Denver who are writers or poets read Gretchen's poems and encouraged us to continue. Jane Carpenter made significant notes, and Pat Paton helped us find people who could give us suggestions; among these were Trista and John Conger. Frank Campbell, a longtime friend and poet, has been an admirer of Gretchen's work for many years.

Gretchen's poetry has been encouraging to families who had a child with Down syndrome. It seemed to give them hope when little was expressed elsewhere. We thank all of you who have encouraged and supported her with your interest.

Meanwhile, Gretchen continues to write whatever message is in her heart.

—*Lula O. Lubchenco*

Foreword

The poetic form allows a connection between poet and reader that is supporting to each. The poetry of Gretchen Josephson is like that. Gretchen reaches out to us, offering her feelings and her observations. Her writing takes us through familiar territory and evokes memories of our own. It is enjoyable to align our remembrances with hers. Many of her poems, though, give us a new view of things. With remarkable economy of words, she brings a fresh spin to common scenes. Most of all, however, she takes us with her on emotional journeys, with diverse themes, that are warmly presented and move us to be grateful for the sharing.

These are poems selected from twenty-five years of Gretchen's composition, beginning in her teens. They provide a panorama of her pleasures, hopes, and concerns, and even some private jokes. She shows us her affection for Christmas, the earth, back doors, home fires, country music, and the Denver Broncos. There are confessions of tears and secrets, of loneliness, of comfort from the Lord. There are precious vacation sites, wonderful family gifts and loyalties, the cherished Denver Dry Goods Department Store, and an agonizing love story. She is no stranger to loss. Gretchen clearly yearns for peace, fairness, and good spirit.

I have been enriched by Gretchen and by her poems. When I read this work to others, they immediately feel the bond. Hence, it is my hope that it can now be experienced by more people. Gretchen's art is uniquely engaging. She is a wry commentator on the human parade. She is hopeful, accepting, generous, and funny. That she has Down syndrome is relevant, of course, but in a gentle, nonpervasive way. There is not a mission in this regard. One can note that life has not always been easy for Gretchen. It is impossible not to love her.

—*Allen C. Crocker*

THIS BOOK IS DEDICATED
    TO my family
MY SISTERS PaTTY Johanna BUNNY
    my MOTHER, Who EDiTS
        MY POETRY
    my faTHER Who GiVes couRege
    and wisdom TO mOVE ON
        AND
    TO DR. CROCKEl
    FOR His FaiTH IN
        MY POETRY

I.

Bus Girl

A Bus Girl Grows Up

How much I have seen!!

I have seen people change
Right before my eyes
Like when they have children.

Old buildings going down
New ones going up

I see people taking an interest
In what they are doing,

Even an Executive talking
With others (shop-talk).

Sometimes I wonder if I can
Be like that (an Executive)
Though I know I never will
Since I'm walking in the steps
Of a Bus Girl.

I think back to the little girl
Walking around
Hanging on to Momie's hand
Walking along Downtown streets
In Sunday clothes, shopping ...

The day is hot
She gets lost
In the Department Store.

But that was when I was little
I don't get lost anymore
And the Department Store is
"The Denver"
The one I'm working in.

I'm not hanging on to Momie's hand
Or getting lost
I've found myself

I belong at the Denver Dry Goods
It's a family of love
The Golden Tea Room

That's why I'm happy to be
Walking in
The steps of a Bus Girl.

A Busy Christmas

"Hustle-Bustle" go the people
Shuffling their feet—
To go to different stores.

"Rattle-Rattle" go the packages
From one arm to the other
Trying to carry the load.
Your arms get tired.

This is as true as the bright lights
Which glow Downtown.
They glow on my face
(as though I were) up with the lights.

As I bus my tables I feel
Deep inside me a confusion
With the Christmas Spirit ...

The decorations in the store I work in
Are beautiful.
But it's not a pudgy man like
Santa Claus so red,
Or the packages under the tree ...

It's the love in the face of our Savior
And love will go with Him forever.

Let us think of Him
In the midst of the confusion
Every year like this.
A busy Christmas!

Heaven's Back Door

I like to remember
My childhood days

Taking my time
Slowly as always
I fumble around for the keys
To the back door
Of our house

Inside there is a fire
That shows love and tenderness
To the ones you love

There is sensitivity
To feelings
And no lack of trust

Back doors are for
Friends and family

I do hope to come through
Heaven's back door

Behind These Eyes

People show or tell what they are
By the look in their eyes.

A man may be inspired by his
Intelligent mind.

Another man shows that he is
Soft and tender.

Behind other eyes you see
A face that is drawn
And looks much older
than he is.

Some eyes are filled with tears
And the face is bronzed
From their sting.

You may see a glow
As bright as the light of the sun.
Behind these are emotions of
Love, faith, admiration and tenderness

Sometimes these eyes show that
They want to talk to others.
And, sometimes, after talking
This person feels better.

Firefly

Fireflies fly all around
And glow all the way
They hum a sweet song ...
(Maybe Country Western, for me)

Their songs may not have lyrics
but someone understands!

I wish I were a Firefly
I would be back in Nashville
I could travel all over,
Even places I was long ago.

They were happy years.
I'd fly away from all the bad things
And tears.

A Firefly does not cry ... Why?
He just loses his glow,
And his halo.

I wish I were a Firefly!

Loneliness

Loneliness is thinking silently when you are
lying in bed.

or watching the moon dipping
more slowly than ever before.

when silence surrounds you
and you are alone,
praying to the Lord.

When you are separating for
the first time.
Some people say "What's the use?"
Some fight, even when you can't win.

Loneliness slowly sinks into you
when you (know you) are not perfect.

Syringes and needles can't cure loneliness
and emptiness
Only understanding and caring will

There is no prescribed medicine
that will cure it
But finding love and contentment will.

Don't lose heart
and faith in yourself.
Find the real you.

Who To Pray To

When I go to bed
I lay awake thinking
In the dark.

The dark is so kind
(It provides privacy)
And also so cruel
(It allows violence)

Laying there thinking
Of tender thoughts
Sends me to sleep.

But then I wonder about
Two men: God and,
Of course, Jesus.

Do they have separate identities
As individuals?
How can they be ONE?

But there is also The Holy Spirit!
It's like a big thick blanket,
Like a down-filled comforter.
It's the Holy Spirit
And it is with us.

Now, I know who to pray to.

Today—I Lost A Friend

Today, I lost a friend
And now it's silence
Through hallways,
Floor after floor
Each one filled with memories

Each one a vision that keeps
Running through my mind

Walking through each corridor,
Personnel, Special Events,
The Restaurant—
Hearing the silence,
All alone

Each floor looks the same
Like an open coffin
Not like the old place of business.
A deafening ringing of silence
In my ears

Still tears are running
Down my face

I may be crying from an inner hurt
I have seen my friends on T.V.
And they share my inner hurt

If you could see the people
I worked for
Looked them in the face
You have seen "The Denver"

Now they turn their heads
And walk away
Not a dry eye left
In the final hours—
They bugged out
For one last time

They closed the story book,
Not a children's tale
It's the one that cost them
Their jobs.

How can we go on now?

We all have been hurt
Nobody can tell me how to feel
Not even family
Who shared my sorrow

My life was there
The place I once stood
And worked for 13 years
Where I left my mark.

We were—and still are
A close knit family
Families gather together
At a time of loss
To mourn the passing of a loved one
With hands coupling together

We sang the songs
That touched our hearts

They buried my friend, today
I read it in the obituary column
In the paper:

*"A department store
closed its doors today."*

The Golden Tea Room
In the sky
Today a friend passed away.

II.

Love for Always

Faith ... Love

You are looking for Love
And searching with a prayer
Of Faith

The Woman
Would be standing
In an open door
Looking for her Man

With a sigh
And a prayer
Her wish comes true

I'm Thinking Of You

When I'm walking
I'm walking with authority,
I hear my foot steps

A half smile is on my face
Because I'm thinking of you
I have a boy on my mind
I'm thinking of you
In a different way

If I'm alone
Don't feel worried about anything
Because I'm with you
No matter where I go

I'm thinking of you

A Face—A Star

A woman is a face—
A star
Into the night

She is a Queen
Shimmering and beautiful
Slender and thin

A girl, a lady, a woman
Life into the night
Is our own

A man tells a woman
You are more than a woman
For you are mine

You should know about young love

Mexican Sunset

As the sun goes down
It shines brightly
Through a window

You see a young girl
Through the golden rays
A Matador walks slowly
Away from the sunset
And into her arms

You said something
In your rusty voice
With tears in your eyes
You draw her closer

Let's look at
The golden sunset
From the top
Of the hill

A Shadow Of A Kiss

A young woman is out with a man
On a date
The sky is dark
But there is a shining,
Shivering cold moon

They are walking
Holding hands
And having a friendly conversation
They are distant from each other

With the dark background
And the moon shining between them
They know how much they care
For each other
They kiss

That's how love is
For the first time

A shadow of a kiss
Could mean marriage
If that's how deep love goes

A shadow of a kiss
How thin is a shadow?
It is like a whisper
or maybe a prayer

A kiss is a way to show
How much you care

An emotion
That never dies

Sweet

In the night
When you wake up crying
Your love is near
Your heart pounds inside you

All you hear outside
Are the birds singing
The stars twinkle
And the moon smiling at you

You are soft
No longer alone in your bed
With your love holding you
Close to him

He will dry your tears
And he will kiss you
During the night

And in silence
Till the night
Starts to break

He will say to you
"I love you"

When The Sun Goes Down

I will see you when
The sun goes down.

I saw you smiling at me
And I smiled at you
Because you saw the sun smile

It's your love
Whispering my name
"I love you Little One"

When I start thinking of you
I see the fire in our souls
For the love we have

It must be a long song
As you see the sunset
And the sunrise
Above the land

I would love to be a dove
Flying over the lush green grass

A clear river or a water fall
With a true blue sky above
And as white clouds in the sky

I will see you
When the sun goes down
I see his face
I hear him

Love And Joy

As a boy and girl
On a misty night
Walking together
We love each other
We kissed

Some thought
We were going to have kids
And think of them
As joy

As far as we know
For certain
We don't need them

Joy is for
The one you love

White Carnation

Behind each fold is
Someone you have been
Waiting for

You see the stars
Twinkle in his eyes

When I have my hair down
In my eyes
I look up and see him

I think of him seriously
And always will

The white carnation says
I Love You

Summer

I don't want to spend
The summer without you
It sounds so silent
Except for the rumbling
In the ground

Or hearing your voice
Ever again
I feel so lonely
Without you

I Will Keep the Home Fires Burning

When I see you near me
I feel the fire
In my soul of love

When I recite poetry
Or soft words
When we kissed each other
For the first time

Or when I saw you
Or you saw me

Even when I'm alone
At home
I will still be with you
Always and forever will

I will always stay open
Late for you
Until the both of us
Will

Keep the home fires burning
For ever

You

The moon is rising
Time is all you need
Take your candle
And leave

My heart is tired
This time you tell me
I'm crying

Today I've seen you
Too much
Leave me here
To pray

Reality

It's a life's story
Trying to make
People understand
What life is

People play different roles
But it will not change life
Or people

It's not how you see it
On T.V.

T.V. makes your problems
Mysterious

Look at them
In the face
See the eyes burning
That must be reality

Kisses into the night—
That's reality

How can we tell other people
About it
And us too?

Sweet Tears

I see the soft waters
Flowing from the spring
The swift waters are
Quiet and deep

Sweet tears are coming
Out of your eyes
When you are talking
To someone

You are thinking a lot
You look into his eyes
And you are starting to cry

Deep down you see
Something is
Caging inside of you

A Tear For My Love

A heart that hurts, Deep inside me
When I'm alone, He is too

This is how I feel about it
My love is true for him
A tear for my love

I see these stars, Look at me
We both had love
In our souls, For each other

If only we can fight this battle of love
Today he is writing a letter of good-bye, It hurts

The love we have is true, If only his mother can see it
If only you can feel, the lump in your throat

Sweet words have been spoken too much
From too many people

Some people think love is a game
It is not—
Not for us two

Is there anybody who can
Mend a broken heart?
Is there anybody who can
Stop these tears?

It's tearing me apart
I'm lonely, why?

Why do we two
Have to suffer?
Why?

What Can I Do To Love Her?

My husband keeps on with
Talk about his mother
What can I do to love her?

She gave life to her son
But now she is refusing
To give it to him
The problem is herself

Really, I need her love
She will never give it
She refused it to everyone

What can I do to love her?
What can I do to help her?
She has had five years
Of hardship
Without love
She's a lonely woman

How can I love her
When she doesn't show it to me?
How can I?

She is lonely
Old
And empty

What can I do?

Soul Fire

I feel lonely and weary
Like a fire when the flames are out
And all that is left is smoke

But it's still burning
That's my soul fire

It keeps burning
It keeps me warm
During the winter
When I'm so lonely

Soul Fire is someone
Who is standing along
Side of you

New Dawn

I'm weeping in my bed
Thinking it's time to rise
In the dark
And falling into the new dawn

I'm thinking about someone
I know, so dear
Who hurt me

I never wanted to be alone
To be alone in the new dawn
Crying in bed

The Bedroom Blues

When I wake up in the morning
I still have tears
running down my face

I rub my eyes
I stumble
My bones creak

When I see the empty bed
And the love that was there

I sure do have

The bedroom blues

God, Have You Seen My Tears?

Lord—our God you have seen
My soul
You have heard me
Talk to you
When I am crying and upset

I have been through
Hard times
Lord, you comfort me

You wiped my tears
With a borrowed Kleenex
God, You have seen my tears

Silence comes over me
I hear your voice
Calling me to come home
And telling me how much
You care for me

The Day I Cried

The day I cried was
When I was separated
From my partner

All the tears need a lake
Big enough to hold them

It's like when someone
Dies in the family
Like when you are losing friends

There's no one to comfort you
You hurt inside

No one seems to do
Anything for you
They turn against you
They deny you
And they differ in opinion

When that happened
I turned to the Lord

When everyone else
Turns away from you
He is the closest friend you have

The day I cried
He was there

Old Memories Never Die

I looked out a bus window, I see a park
With nobody in it

I have the vision, of a young couple
Holding hands and walking in the park

They are walking into the flame of a candle
Reflections come into both minds of Love
Old memories never die!

You grieve—as with death
You feel—lost

You look for comfort, a hug
That says "It's all right I'm here"

You hear the silence, The still of the night
and the longing of the days
You thumb through pictures and old things
and you find out
That love never dies!

What went wrong?
Maybe I failed at Love
You can see where I'm in doubt

You can't predict Love
You can be Loving Blind

You can see the hurt on my face
You can see I'm not smiling

But I wonder
If I can find it again
Will old memories never die?

III.

*Vacations
& Travel*

What You Can Learn From a Seagull

At Carter Lake I watched
The thin earth
With the water covering the beach

I stared up at the sky
And watched the seagulls fly
Making music

Listening to the peace
Just to hear them singing
As they glide through the air

They tell us when there's a
Change in the weather

The sky of soft colors
That's just normal
The weather feels good

They just mourn in the night
And cry themselves to sleep

Reflection

I was walking in the woods
And found this clearing
Water dripping down
In this wooded ravine

I found a pond of water
Which reminded me of yesterday
I saw the reflection of love

I saw a reflection of sunshine
And a golden ring
I saw my own reflection
Wishing for a man by my side

I could feel the cold water
On my face
And rushing through my fingers
Like the mountain dew

I sat on the banks
Staring into the pond

I could see my face
As in a mirror
And wondered
Why am I here?

Weeping Willow

The willow tree cries
The branches hang straight down
And cry into the breeze

The crying never stops
There must be a time
To dry up

The tree sheds its leaves
In the fall
And becomes crisp and crunchy
In the winter

That's the way it is
Like a person
Hanging on a limb
for dear life

Going into sudden death
Or withering away
And life goes on
Beyond that

For a weeping willow
The cycle is endless
Life never stops
And that's beautiful

I Love My Country Ways

When I hear country music
It takes me back
To when I was growing up

It's running on the beach
At Pawley's Island

It's swimming in the ocean
And feeling the warm rain
With not a care in the world.

Sometimes the country songs
make me think of loved ones
Who have passed away
And how that brings families together.

This poem will go on forever
And so will the songs.

They will pick up the beat and tempo
Love will grow stronger
With each heart beat
Of life.

A Final Wyoming

These were happy years
To lose them was like losing
Something close to you

The pain is always there
Just like death
In the family

The family is always there
Memories are always there

There is a final for everything
—The ending of a song
—The fading of lights
—The fading away from life

But memories are for always
The song is endless
Like love

Farewell To Wyoming: Remembrance

I remember sticking my head
Out of the trailer door

It was raining

So I looked out of the window
At the river
You could hear
The rushing sound

On the barbed wire fence
Sat a huge bird
Could it be a bald eagle?

The river poured over its bank
And filled the creek

Grandmother Mom was a sight
To see crossing over
The makeshift bridge

One night Mama wanted me
To cook dinner
The stove blew up
Papa was inside reading the paper
When he heard the loud bang
It was pretty near dark outside
Terry, Hanny, Mama, Patty, Bunny
Were coming home from fishing
What would their expressions be?

Papa woke up us kids one morning
With the noise of a chain saw
So I yelled back something
About his making music
—Country Music!

And Papa's big fish story!
These were happy years.

I remember the lush green meadows
Getting caught in the ruts
On rocky and muddy roads
When it rained
I rain too
When I think about it

We usually went up to Wyoming
For my birthday
Once I got a cheese cake
Down at work at The Denver
A car with a canoe on top
Stopped for me

My friends looked at each other
Like "What's that?"
One said "That's JR's folks"
What a laugh they had'

Laughter and tears
Go hand in hand
Tears speak louder than words
Bitter-sweet tears
Those are mine!

I Left My Tears In Wyoming

From the morning
I poked my head out of the door
And heard the rushing water

To the many birthdays
I celebrated there
As I grew up

I will always think of Wyoming
It was my corner of the world
It was a time of happiness

For closing thoughts
I would say it
Through a song

Books have to end sometimes
We are riding off into the sunset

No matter where I'm dreaming
I can see a long valley
With fences going on for miles
I guess life will go on forever

I realized that I should
Leave my tears
In Wyoming
And remember the good times

Now
I want to spend
My birthday
With my friends
At The Denver

Flight Of A Bald Eagle

If only you could capture
The beauty of a bird

Trace his pattern in flight
His majesty, his boldness

He is erect
The flight of a bald eagle

Sometimes it is their last flight
Soaring into the sky

One hears their cry
For help
And they fall
Beside a busy highway

Lying dead
A pitiful sight
A tragedy
Of a beautiful bird

We must save them
So there won't be that night

Southern Memories

I remember being at Pawley's Island
collecting clams
We tried to open them with a hammer
But the head fell off

Alice had her guitar on the beach
She lost her contacts in the sand
She must have a heart ache

Hanny was in the dance hall
but I was sick with a cold
Papa gave me cough medicine

I remember picking up sea shells
Hearing the sea rumble
Softly in my ears
Then I saw the sunset

I was in the ocean
so many times!

As I went in
Here came the breakers
Took me back to shore
Then I ran back out
I wish I hadn't

My eyes were pouring salt
They still do
As I can't stop thinking of Pawley's

I will remember it always
Those sweet memories

Pawley's Island Love Call

I can see the line
    in the sand
I can hear the roar
    of the ocean
I am seeing the waves
    coming and going

I can hear
    Pawley's Island love call

I am seeing
    my relatives
We are singing
    the songs of yesterday
And telling stories
    just like yesterday.

I can still taste
    the ocean
And feel
    the salt in my eyes.
And yearning
    to turn back time.
Pawley's Island
    always draws you back.

You are walking
    on the beach
Or being grounded
    by a wave

You feel the undertow
    between your toes.
You feel the draw
    that makes your legs weak,
    and takes you down
You see the blue sky overhead
It's a call
    the Pawley's Island love call

In the background
    is the roar of the ocean
There are hugs and kisses
    before leaving
In your eyes
    the salt burns,
You are standing alone
    but you have to go on.

You look everywhere,
    you look into
    nooks and crannies
    lakes and rivers
    open fields
    woods and mountains,
But you never find it.

There's only one
    Pawley's Island.

Italy

The remembrance of Italy
The visions of it
I can stop what I am doing
Just to visualize this for a long time

The long hallways
The sacred churches
The steeple of Saint Peter's Basilica

The water and the lakes of Venice
Walking along on cobble stone streets
In the rain

It's very refreshing
But leaves you empty and lonely

The warmth of Milan
That meets the flowing of tears
And pulling of heart strings
I feel close to these people

I watched the people of Italy
How they dip their fingers in the water
And made the sign of
The Father, Son, and Holy Ghost

When you see the little ones
Speaking Italian
That's when I cry

When you walk through the churches
On marble floors
You feel the silence overwhelm you

Hearing the history of Italy
Makes me wonder all the more
What life is all about

The Beauty of Planet Earth

When I saw Planet Earth photographed
I was wondering
As most people would

It is the black sky
With the colorful planet
Coloring the sky

When the sun shines
Above the clouds
I wonder if the clouds are
suspended?

When I am above the clouds
This is where I am satisfied
Because that to me
Is being perfect

From an airplane
They look like mountains
Where you can touch them

Its breathtaking beauty
Surrounds you

The clouds are like
Ice and snow
The barren beauty of winter

One day I will look up
Into the sky
And wonder why?

IV.

Family

The Warmness Of A Mother
(My mother)

She will have a low hum
Sweet as her perfume
A warm touch of her hand.

There is tenderness in everything
She touches
It brings back life

She shows life in everything
She does.

In her line of work with little ones,
Like newborns
She understands their cries
It's their way to show emotion.

It makes me cry when I see
My mother, a doctor,
Holding a child and talking to her
Like she was one of her own.

She brings love and tenderness
And warmth
Into the hospital.

Inspiration of a Man

An inspiration of a man
Who has wisdom, courage and faith
Sometimes he makes you feel good
And you look up to him

I see Papa in his early years
Going to work
Dressed up like an executive
Looking like the Chairman of the Board
And being proud of it

The inspiration of a man, like Papa,
Gave me strength
To be a good steward

He could be jovial or in a joking mood
When he is like this
He twinkles his eyes at me
And starts laughing
That's when I chime in

His other mood is confusing
Sometimes he presses the panic button

When he does this
He yells from the top of the stairs
He makes me cry
He sounds like one of my bosses at work

I love my father
But sometimes I wonder about him

To get ahead in life
Papa would say
"Don't back down
When your back is against the wall"

Papa has shown me when to be strong
And when to be tender and compassionate

I wouldn't know what I would do
If something happened to him

Leaving

Mama said to leave the light on
And lock the door
When I leave

It's safer that way
No burglars can sneak in
To steal that which is dear

If that happens
Let us never go bitter
Till hate rots away

I'd rather have
The happy things
we've shared

A Birthday Poem

I know this lady
And her husband
They had three children
And lived in a foreign land

Her children were playing
And running in a cotton field
Having fun

One day they came home
for lunch
The table was set
With fine china and silver

Suddenly, they packed
a few belongings
And left this nation
In a war of turmoil

They found themselves
In the United States
And lived in the south

But now they are with
Their own family and friends

One of their children is unique
In every way
Because she gave birth on this date
August 25th 1954
 "To Me"

Much love,
Your daughter and friend
Gretchen

My Father—My Friend

There is a song I love
"I guess it never hurts to hurt sometime"

Every time I hear it
I think of one person—
My father.

It reminds me of going to and from work
When the sky is blue
And he is "up there"
Guiding me every day.

From the exterior he was bold
His inspiration was in his work
His admiration was in his family
and friends.

His tenderness sometimes
brought tears

When something happened
And you needed him
You found out that
He was a part of your life.

My father—My friend

The Retirement Waltz

You see two people
Loving each other
For more years than they ever expected

They found retirement
Hard to do
There was turmoil
And emptiness

These two people I love—
My folks

They never thought they would
Have a past to give them
A retirement waltz

V.

Death
& Grief

The Sting of Death

Why is there the sting of death?
Sometimes there is no answer
It just happens

It is like a bee sting
You don't get over it
It drives you
Into a pool of tears

It is like you are sick
And empty
And there's nothing you can do about it

Too many questions about life.

But there is one thing about death ...
There are people who deal with it every day
Who can help
Sometimes these persons are ministers,
Physicians, funeral directors

Why is there the sting of death?
The burning in the eyes?
The jerking of heart strings?
The memories ... ?

Grandmother Mom—A Tribute

She grew sleek and slender
Into a beautiful woman
And still is

She had wisdom as a child and
She had knowledge
Like nobody else had

She never spoke an unkind word
To anyone
Because she loved them
No matter who they were
It was heart warming

She became a doctor
Her hands were skilled
She gave her life to be one

She always loved flowers
Even up to the end
"when the Lord calls me"

Flowers were a part of her life
She saw beauty in people too
And lived by this prayer

She had a smile for everyone
Even for family
Every one admired her

As for me,
She was my Grandmother
I say this with
Tears in my eyes

Because the memory is so great
Because I will always love her

She will always be
A friend
I never forget a friend
Like her

This song, these lines
Come from the heart
They will never be duplicated

The First Christmas Without Papa

Last Christmas was a silent one
It was looking at pictures
of what once was
and you were not there

You are among friends
peers and colleagues at work
And you turn away because
you do not want them to know
how you feel

You feel empty, lonely
And in despair
You don't hear the children
Playing, laughing or crying

You don't see the beauty
Of holiday joy
Or the birds and squirrels
Amid the snow

All you hear is silence,
Sorrow and grief
You are closed off
to the world

You look back over your shoulders
And you see only the past

A father is important to his family
Think of all you have
And how precious you are
See the beauty in your children
And the wonder in their eyes
See them for what they are

A Christmas Memory of Papa

I can see Papa putting up a Christmas tree
Stringing the lights up and out
    and checking them
One by one

And Papa going with us
To deliver poinsettias
To friends and patients

Also putting the lights up
On the trees
Outside of the house

I remember the time
We had the psychedelic Christmas
Strobe lights, loud music,
and slides

There was a banner that said
"MERRY CHRISTMAS'
And us kids dancing around
The Christmas tree

Can you imagine
Mama's and Papa's
Reaction to this scene?

On Christmas morn
When we woke up
There were presents
    at the fireplace
and the first phone call
you would answer by saying
"Christmas Gift"

One Christmas we spent at a ski lodge
We used the sauna
Then rolled in the snow

For New Years we all showed slides
And someone picked the winning slide
Howard always showed a barn on fire
And Mama's close-up was a rose

While we waited for the New Year
We made resolutions
And at midnight we got out
The pots and pans
And banged them senseless

On New Year's day
We celebrated with fire works
While the men sat
Burning the tube with football
And yelling at the same time

P.S.
This poem is to my father,
but it could be to all fathers.
Be grateful that you have one.
(Written on the 5th anniversary of his death)

VI.

Faith

Prayer

Lord
Sometimes I feel guilty
For some things I do

Will you forgive me
For anything I do wrong?

I feel out of conversations
I feel I am not wanted
I'm alone and in the blues

If you can help me
I will thank you for it
When I see you

Living with God's Children
in Difficult Times

Our Minister says
"We are all God's Children"
But living with "God's Children"
Is difficult at times

For instance, terrorists
All they know is how to start wars
Do they care how many tears have been shed?
Do they know what peace is?

Some of "God's Children"
Use power and prestige
They use people
Then throw them away

Some are rude and violent
Some are crazed and do weird things

Some physically harm
Family and loved ones

It is hard to forgive
Time is said to heal
But life is too short
Healing is a slow process
Sometimes it takes a lifetime
of being human

VII.

Other Poems

Peace

I'm just sitting here
At the breakfast-nook table
And hearing
The crying of the teapot.

Just thinking to myself ...
If only we can have peace here
And everywhere.

But all I hear is
The crying of our men.

The Crisis of a Modern Woman

She goes to the grocery store
Pushes the cart
Up and down the aisles
Planning meals

She goes to the produce
And meat sections
"Rump or chuck?"

How to pick out melons?
She thumps, smells, and shakes them
And hopes the seeds rattle inside

She goes to the office
Her desk is a fright
Her boss is complaining
About reports

There may be a board meeting
Only minutes away

Have you made the coffee yet ?

Then she goes home
To her husband and children

She's married
But to whom?
Her job or her family?

There are children to care for
And to educate
And a husband to love

What happens if one of them
Becomes ill?

This liberated woman
Steps out in style
Where is she going?

To give a speech?
A fund raiser?
Or with her husband?

You may call this woman
A liberated woman
She may have political power
She has equal rights

But is this so?
I don't know

A Retailer's Nightmare

It's the Christmas season
He hears buzzers going off
Indicating security problems
He sees kids racing off

Cash registers ring
Bells jingle outside the door
Too many bells going off in his head

There are advertisements to do
Layouts, sketches, fashion trends of today
And new styles to consider.
So much paper work

He must keep people on their feet
Deal with angry customers

He must keep in touch with colleagues
Getting advice, or a second opinion
What is the right decision for his company?
Can he do all this?

Behind Retailing

When you are taking out merchandise
To hang on the rack
Or when you are going down
To get supplies
You wonder—

When you close your eyes
You can see the semi-trailer rigs
Going down the highway
At a fast clip

You can feel the rumble
Under the ground
You can hear the semi
Putting on his horn

He passes bill boards
Like advertising and food
He looks at the painted lines
Double yellow or white

Even in the darkest rain
With head lights on
Smoke stacks blaring
He is bolting down the highway

In the darkest night
He sees the biggest cities
The smallest towns
With lights that look like
Computer circuitry

When he reaches our dock
He waits impatiently
For the freight elevator

Fading Away Into Old Memories

It's like a country singer
When he is done performing
Fading away from the lights

Or it's like going through old albums
Pictures fade and become distorted
in colors and shapes
Thinking of people I dearly miss

You can drown your tears
In sorrow and see the blues
Or fade away into old memories

Death gets you this way, too
It shows you that you are not that strong
That people don't bounce back that quickly
It takes time, and hurts inside

It seems endless
It will keep on forever
Fading into old memories

Leave Me Here

Leave me here
I'm about to see the world
The gray and dusky sky

To turn against the wind
The cold winter burns my face

To turn to my friends and loved ones
For love

Leave me here
To suffer the sword of love

For this is my life
I have no love of my own
But for others I do
My family and friends

A Blue Christmas

This young woman has lost her parents
And she faces life alone

She is also expecting
Her husband is standing next to her

He is like Joseph
And she is (today's) Mary

They go to Lamaze classes
They stay in a homeless shelter
She gives birth to their son

It is a blue Christmas
When a babe is born from a mother
Of a broken marriage
And is trying to raise a child without a father
Struggling for love

Or when
A young girl walks the streets at night
Walks by a hospital
In a deep depression
Walks in and goes up to the wing
Where the tiny little ones are
Especially when Christmas comes

The Crying Of A Steel Guitar

On a stage, shining
Under a blue flood light
Is a free standing steel guitar

Soon there will be sounds
Twanging of strings
Sliding of the bar
And old country songs
Or old gospel songs
Will be heard

You can hear the crying
From the steel guitar
The blues from a man
Walking the streets
Or the cry from a broken heart

Sometimes the voice is hollow
Sometimes shallow
Sometimes a lonesome belle
Sobbing in the dark

The lark in the sky says
"Why?"
"Why do you cry?"

When Love Stops Hurting

When you have loved someone
Love never stops hurting
You will do anything for love

Is it really for love?

If love never stops hurting
You are hurting yourself
You feel numb
Like "Is this really happening?"

You feel empty, depressed
Just like before you start to cry

But tears never flow
You cover your face with your hands
You feel the rushing of the river
Going over rocks
Floods and streams
With no one to turn to

When you find a friend
Then love stops hurting

Convicted

I am in a court room
There sits a judge
There is a jury
And a testifying booth

You see,
by looking into my eyes
Pain and sorrow
And hurt

You are dressed all in white
Walking across the room

You can visualize yourself
In jail
A young person
Clutching onto the bars
Staring into space

You are convicted of LOVE

Sometimes you wonder
What love is all about
Isn't love a lesser charge than
A sentence to life?

No love is greater
Than the gift of life

Heart Of Steel
Cold As Stone

Sometimes it's someone you love
The hurt is deeper
And the trust is gone

How can love last
When he turns away?
Or he testifies against you?
Or finds another woman?

It may be a time of rage
You can't predict love
From a man with a heart of steel

Maybe I failed at love
Maybe I was taken in
Maybe I was yearning
And needed to be caressed?

I'm not smiling now
I wonder—can I find love again?

Mabel
(My music teacher)

My music teacher plays the violin
She also plays in the Symphony
She teaches persons with disabilities

She teaches for the love
of music
She teaches discipline
And perseverance

She knows this will grow
within us

We are the flowers
in her garden
She sees the beauty
in her yard

We will be in harmony
in her music

And after the lesson
She waits for a hug

God's Speed

People often say "Godspeed to you my son"
It shows that they love them.

Sometimes the saying
Has me wondering—?

What speed does God have?
Fast or slow?
Country or rock and roll?

God's speed does not
Pick up the tempo
With the music.
God's speed is silent.

God's speed has only one speed
And it's for all of
God's children

God's speed is mysterious
The answer to it is still mysterious.
Someday we may find out.

Statue Of Liberty

The Statue of Liberty stands tall
Slender and erect
Above the city

She overlooks harbors
With barges going by

She holds a torch of freedom
She is molded into clay and cement
She feels the coolness of the night
And the blistering heat of the day

She looks down on the people
Businessmen, New York officials
And the poor and rich alike

Her face is bronzed
And she weeps over the city

Her torch burns
Not only for freedom
But for Peace and Love

Every city should have a
Statue of Liberty

Hope
Peace
Love and
Freedom

Orange Fever
(A fairy tale)

I went to the doctor
With a strange ailment

He found out that it was a
Common, but local disease

No, it's not cancer
No, it's not heart disease

"Oh—I have a fever?"
Yes, it's Orange Fever!

It gets you up
Raring to go
It's like a car with cruise control

I was driving a car
Traffic was bumper to bumper
People were irate
And I was swerving
In and out of lanes

A cop pulled me over
To give me a ticket
But I told him I had a fever
And had to get somewhere

I had to get to the game!!
"Not the Bronco game??"
"Yes, it's Orange Fever"

He told me to follow him
Forget about the ticket
And get well soon

About the Author

Gretchen L. Josephson was born in Denver, Colorado, on August 25, 1954, the fourth child (and also the fourth daughter) of Lula Lubchenco and Carl Josephson. She was born with Down syndrome, but had no serious medical problems. During her early years she received speech therapy and was enrolled in a preschool for about one year. She attended special education classes in the Denver public school system.

By the time she was in junior high school, Gretchen was writing poetry. When she wrote "Peace," it became apparent that she was acutely aware of and troubled by the war in Vietnam and was expressing these feelings through her writing.

Gretchen's first job was working as a bus girl in a downtown department store, the Denver Dry Goods Tea Room. This restaurant was an elite downtown luncheon place revered by Denver citizens. Gretchen wrote "Bus Girl" and the poems that follow it during a rather difficult period in her life, which included moving to an apartment and a failed love affair. Her work was the one stable factor in her life. She was brokenhearted when the store closed, and pours out her anguish in "Today—I Lost A Friend."

Gretchen met a young man during her last year of high school. Their attraction for each other quickly developed into a love affair. She used her poetry to describe her feelings of love, disappointment, and despair when their dreams did not come true.

Gretchen's life has been full with work, travel, church, and other community activities. She draws on all these experiences in her writing. She expresses her feelings—sometimes happy moments, sometimes sad ones; occasionally it is curiosity or puzzlement about things she doesn't quite understand.

More recently she has moved to her own apartment. She continues to write, both poetry and prose. There is a wide range of interest in her poems, and a curiosity about the world in which she lives. People still dominate her thoughts, especially country music artists and their songs.

—Lula O. Lubchenco